LYRIC SOPRANO ARIAS
A Master Class with
EVELYN LEAR

Recorded Master Classes on Nine Arias • Recorded Piano Accompaniments

Interpretive Essays • Extensive Coaching Comments in the Score of each Aria

Robert L. Larsen, pianist
study translations by Martha Gerhart

ED 4240
Originally released in book/cassette form.

ISBN 0-634-09840-3

G. SCHIRMER, Inc.

DISTRIBUTED BY

T0052399

Contents

The Companion CDs

CD 1

CD 2

Dear Fellow Artist,

It seems just yesterday that I was starting my own performing career. I remember so vividly my first audition. How terrifying it was!

I know what it is like to be in your shoes. I know how frustrating it is to feel the music inside of you, and not know how to communicate that music, through your voice, to an audience. The reason for this volume is to help you to discover the best method of communicating your art and fulfilling your musical desires.

For this book I have chosen what I believe are the nine arias most fundamental to a lyric soprano's repertory. In fact, I can't imagine that any soprano could live through her college years without learning at least a few of these arias. I've included arias in Italian, French, German, and English, representing composers from Handel to Puccini, and, of course, quite a few Mozart arias. We all know how instructive, yet challenging it is to sing Mozart's music. It keeps a young singer's voice well-oiled.

One of the great joys of my life is giving master classes to young singers. They fuel me with their eagerness and enthusiasm, and inspire and challenge me to sift through all my years of performing and teaching to come up with accurate advice for each of them. When I began preparing this volume of lyric soprano arias, I had to reshape my comments from the way I normally conduct my master classes. Rather than advising individuals (as I do in my formal master classes), some of my ideas and advice became more generalized, but will apply to any soprano who sings these arias.

The recorded sessions, the essays, and the coaching comments are all designed as suggestions for each artist to consider. I have tried to stay away from advice that is too specifically geared toward one singer. In the recorded master class sessions I have chosen to work with talented, college-age sopranos, rather than with finished young professionals. These young women are, I think, typical of those many students at colleges and universities who might best benefit from the kind of study I recommend. After all, it is at that time of your life when you begin to study these familiar arias, and it is important to create healthy working habits. I feel, however, that the recorded and printed lessons on each aria will be appropriate for students beyond those first college years as well.

I hope that my ideas about the performing of these great pieces of music will help you to communicate vividly what you are deeply feeling as you sing them. One point that I have stressed again and again is that you must speak the text of your music frequently so that you understand what it is that you are saying and feeling. The following progression is absolutely vital to a convincing performance:

1. Read and think the text without speaking it out loud. Understand it and put it into your own words.

2. Allow yourself to feel deeply what you are reading.

3. Speak the text out loud, freely, not in rhythm. Then speak it in the rhythm of the music.

4. Sing through the melody of the aria without words, *mezza voce.*

5. Now you are allowed to put text and melody together to sing and perform.

These master class sessions were originally recorded in 1990 and released on cassette. I am thrilled that these lessons are now available, much more conveniently to students, on the two CDs included with this book.

I hope that I have helped you to discover some pertinent ideas that will aid you in making these arias your very own. Only through dedicated study can you bring them to life in a personal, artistic and satistfying way. Coraggio!

Very sincerely yours,

Evelyn Lear
Ft. Lauderdale, Florida
July, 2005

Evelyn Lear with Robert L. Larsen and the college student sopranos featured on the CD (1990).

Introduction

by Evelyn Lear

There is so much to think about and to learn as a performer, that it's always difficult to know where to start and when to stop when working with young artists. I've spent hours and hours working with singers in master classes, and yet I realize at the end of each session that I had just gotten started.

Before I begin to work with the arias I've chosen to include in this volume, I'd like to discuss some general issues about performing. In my introductory comments on the CD, I discussed ideas about learning music and making it your own. How do you interpret the music after you've done all your preparation and study? You get up before an audience and you sing, of course.

The first thing that I believe that is absolutely crucial is to realize that from the moment you walk on to a stage—be it a recital, concert, or opera—it becomes theater, it becomes magic. It's up to you to prepare yourself so that you are worth the attention your audience gives you. Backstage, you can do anything you need to get yourself ready. Some performers do breathing exercises or pace around. Some close their eyes and intensely turn inward. Some pray. Some seem to be bouncing off the walls because of the excess nervous energy. In short, you're likely to see performers doing anything and everything backstage before they enter the stage, and that's the way it should be. But the moment you enter, all of that activity is left backstage.

You must know who you are. You must become the character that you are about to present. If you are on the opera stage, you must *be* in that character. If you are on the concert stage, you must have carriage and grace that is worthy of the audience's attention. Don't rush on as if you are afraid that if you don't start singing right away the audience will leave! Many student singers enter that way: quickly, ashamedly, timidly. No! You must understand that the audience is captive, and is there for you. Have the confidence in yourself and your role as a performer to make a dignified entrance. You might think of your whole body as a type of ship that is gracefully sailing into place, calmly, serenely. You have a unique gift, and a special secret that you are about to share with them. You must make them feel that. Do not apologize in your attitude, in your mental state, or in your posture. Do not apologize for being there. Remember, it's really a privilege to be on stage in front of people. A privilege that you, and only you are granted at that moment by your talent, your voice, and the musical message that you are there to bring. Relish the moment!

I've been on stage all my life and I can tell you that you must continually have this kind of high regard and respect for both your audience and especially for yourself. Each time you perform you must renew these feelings within yourself, or they become old and stale. And you must understand that not only is each audience different, but also that each time you perform you are a different person than you were the last time you performed, even if it was only yesterday. You have no choice but to continually recreate yourself as a performer. Each time you encounter an audience is a fresh adventure. Remember that.

All of this internal work is important to make a total impression. You must work on your voice, on your musicianship, on the grace with which you portray the music. Study your languages, make them your own. Take German, or French, or Italian phrases and put them into your own words in English and say them naturally. Recite your texts as if they were a dramatic recitation long before you ever sing them. This is absolutely essential.

If you do your best, you will succeed as a communicative artist. Do it with love, with dedication, and with lots of patience.

Biography

EVELYN LEAR, internationally celebrated soprano, sang more than 40 operatic roles in the great opera houses of the world. She appeared as a star with virtually every major opera company in the United States, from the Metropolitan Opera to San Francisco Opera, and in Europe has appeared at La Scala, Covent Garden, the Paris Opera, Vienna State Opera, the Canadian Opera, in Buenos Aires with Teatro Colón, and in Berlin, Hamburg, and Munich, among countless other locales. Miss Lear has also appeared in all the world's major festivals, from Edinburgh, Holland, Salzburg, Munich, and Florence to Tanglewood, Ravinia, Blossom, Aspen, and the Hollywood Bowl.

A native of Brooklyn, New York, Miss Lear was educated at Hunter College, New York University, and the Juilliard School, where she studied piano, composition, French horn, percussion, and voice. In 1957 a Fulbright Fellowship enabled her to study at the Hochschule für Musik in Berlin. In 1959 she became a member of the Berlin Opera Company, where her first performance was as the Composer in *Ariadne auf Naxos*, a role she later repeated at Vienna, Hamburg, Munich, and the Metropolitan Opera. In 1960, on three weeks notice, Miss Lear learned the title role in Alban Berg's *Lulu* for the Austrian premiere (in concert form) in Vienna. The performance proved so successful that the first staged version since World War II was presented at Theater an der Wien during the Vienna Festival of 1962, with Miss Lear in the title role, under the baton of Karl Böhm. In 1965 she made her Covent Garden debut as Donna Elvira in *Don Giovanni*. That same year Miss Lear was invited to make her American debut as Cleopatra in Handel's *Giulio Cesare* at the gala opening of the Kansas City Performing Arts Center, as well as her debut at the San Francisco Opera as Lulu. In 1966 she made her Lyric Opera of Chicago debut as Poppea in Monteverdi's *L'Incoronazione di Poppea*. Evelyn Lear's debut with the Metropolitan Opera came in 1967 when she created the role of Lavinia in the world premiere of Levy's *Mourning Becomes Elektra*. In the meantime, she was in constant demand throughout the world repeating her success in *Lulu*, and appearing in a repertoire that also included *Bluebeard's Castle, La bohème, The Merry Widow, Die Zauberflöte, Otello, Falstaff, Eugene Onegin, Tosca, Don Giovanni, Boris Godunov, Così fan tutte,* and many other operas.

Miss Lear is the only American artist in history to have performed the three principal female roles in *Der Rosenkavalier* (Sopie, Octavian, the Marschallin).

Miss Lear's extensive discography includes several complete operas. *Der Rosenkavalier, Wozzeck, Die Zauberflöte* among the most notable. Her 33 recordings also include lieder, oratorio, orchestral repertoire, duets, American songs, and further operatic ventures. She also appeared as Nina Cavallini in the 1974 Robert Altman film *Buffalo Bill and the Indians*, and starred in a musical in New York entitled *Elizabeth and Essex*, in which she portrayed Elizabeth I. Miss Lear has become a renowned master class artist, with memorable classes given to young artists at Juilliard, Music Academy of the West, Oberlin Conservatory, Saint Louis Opera, Santa Fe Opera, Manhattan School of Music, Canadian Opera, Rotterdam Conservatory, Des Moines Metro Opera, and many other venues. She is married to Thomas Stewart, leading bass-baritone.

ROBERT L. LARSEN, pianist for the recorded accompaniments, is founder and artistic director of one of America's major summer opera festivals, the Des Moines Metro Opera, and serves as both conductor and stage director for all the company's productions. He is respected as a much sought after opera coach, and has worked with countless professional singers with important operatic careers. Since 1965 he has been chairman of the department of music at Simpson College in Indianola, Iowa, and has established a serious and extensive program of operatic training for undergraduates at the college. He is editor of the *G. Schirmer Opera Anthology,* the world's most widely used source of arias, and other key publications. Dr. Larsen holds a bachelor's degree from Simpson College, a master's degree in piano performance from the University of Michigan, and a doctorate degree in opera conducting from Indiana University.

The recording was made January 12-13, 1990 at Simpson College. The Simpson student sopranos featured on the recording are Rita Harvey, Beth Cummins, Traci Smith, Julie Poe, and Mari Marroquin.

Let the bright Seraphim

from *Samson*
music by George Frideric Handel

This has become one of the most famous and festive soprano arias in the repertory. In the plot of the oratorio, the blinded Samson, having been tricked and betrayed by his wife, Dalila, is held captive by the Philistines. He is faithful to Jehovah, the Lord God of Israel, in the face of his captors' zealous loyalty to the pagan god Dagon. Led by his faith, he answers the Philistines' demand to exhibit his strength by destroying their temple to Dagon, burying himself and his enemies in the ruins. Samson's Israelite friends gravely mourn his death, but after a time the mood changes to celebration when they declare him victorious in his martyrdom. An Israelite woman then sings this brilliant aria in celebration of Samson's martyrdom. Technically an oratorio, *Samson* has been regularly and effectively presented in fully staged productions by opera companies. The libretto is after the poet Milton's *Samson Agonistes*, which is, of course, based on the biblical story of Samson.

In the context of the oratorio, the aria ends after the B section, without a *da capo*. However, when performed on its own, the aria needs a *da capo* for formal resolution. The piece is very effective when performed with a solo trumpet, and we have included the trumpet part in this edition. There is no readily available edition of the aria in piano reduction that presents this wonderful trumpet part, and I felt strongly that this should be part of this collection. If you perform the aria with trumpet, rehearse enough so that you feel very closely knit as an ensemble. There's an exhilirating satisfaction when you "click" with other musicians in creating a perfect ensemble. This is especially true in the quick *fioratura* in parallel thirds.

Unlike other arias in this collection, "Let the bright Seraphim" can work for an audience and a performer as a stand-alone piece, without knowing anything about the plot or character context of the aria within *Samson*. However, I do strongly urge you to study this context, at least for your own professional integrity.

How often do we get to sing standard, pre-20th century literature in English? Handel and Purcell comprise almost the complete active repertory of this genre, with few other additions. Relish this opportunity. Take this stylized English text and roll it around on your tongue until it feels noble, natural and beautiful. Don't make the obvious mistake of assuming that since the aria is in your native language of English that you will not have to work on diction and language delivery. On the contrary, you need to work to uplift the diction of the sung text out of your everyday speaking habits. There are many things to ponder in this regard. In this case, take particular care that the pronunciation is crisp and British, not American, since that is the music's place of origin. Flip and roll your R's in the proper style.

This aria is as celebratory a piece of music as a soprano will ever sing. Your presentation has to match the excitement that is built into the music. One of the wonders of musical art is that it can sustain emotion in a beautiful, stylized way. This masterful music by Handel is really a shout of joy that is far more sustained, profound and resonant than any literal shout could ever be.

I have suggested some conservative *da capo* ornamentation for the aria. There is a great deal of freedom in designing this kind of thing, and you are certainly free to disregard my suggestions and come up with your own. My general advice is to remember that you are decorating an existing melody. You are not creating a new melody, nor a descant to the existing melody. If the ornamentation is overdone, the audience may hear it as an unattractive display of egotism by the singer. I have suggested a brilliant scale up to a high D for the final cadenza, with an alternate that avoids going that high. But by all means, rewrite the cadenza to suit your own voice.

Let the bright Seraphim

from *Samson*

George Frideric Handel

Play the bass line slightly detached throughout.

You should feel as if the introduction is expressing your ecstatic inner mood.

Trumpet

An Israelite Woman:

Flip all "R's" at the beginning of syllables.

Let the bright Se - ra - phim in

*Small size notes in the piano part are to be played only when there is no trumpet soloist.

Experiment with singing the 2 16th notes in the pattern with distinct accents.

burn - ing row, in burn - ing, burn - ing row, their

A baroque style luftpause is optional here.

Carefully tune the octave leap up to this phrase.

slightly marcato

loud, up - lift - ed an - gel trum - pets blow, _____ their

luftpause necessary

loud, up - lift - ed an - gel trum - pets blow, _____

* A "luftpause" (breathing rest) can be a stylistic feature in lines such as this that spill into coloratura.

Make certain that the breaths happen exactly in tempo, exactly on beat 4, and are exactly equivalent to 16th note rests.

Keep the melisma energized, with a subtle feeling of crescendo throughout. The beat must remain constant.

Do not disrupt the tempo in taking the breath.

cresc.   crescendo to cut off

If you need a breath here, place it exactly on beat 4 with an 8th rest duration.

their loud, _____ their

You may want to round and lengthen the a vowel in "angel" in high spots to avoid a strident sound.

loud, up - lift - ed an - gel trum - pets blow,

let the bright Se - ra - phim in

burn - ing row, in burn - ing, burn -

*Keep the tempo steady
the first time through.*

- ing row, their loud, up - lift - ed;

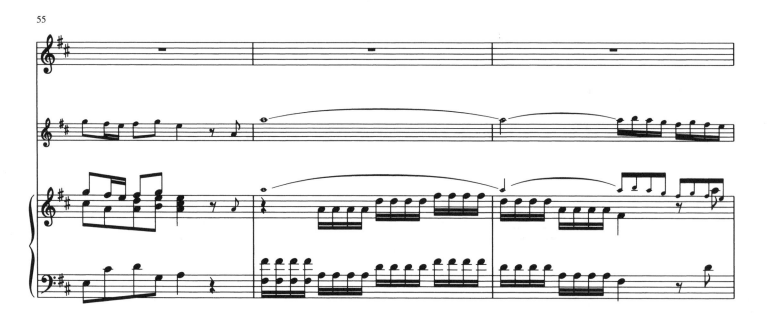

Keep this energized, even
though it's softer.

An appoggiatura is effective on
the 2nd syllable of "tuneful."

An "e" rather than D# is often
sung on the 2nd syllable of "golden."

* I like the idea of keeping the B section right in tempo in this case, but many performers slow this section down,
sometimes drastically so.

73

(opt. rit.)

* (tr) (a tempo)

harps ____ with gold - en wires.

Trumpet

77

80 *Once again, remember that this music is expressing your inner ecstatic mood.*

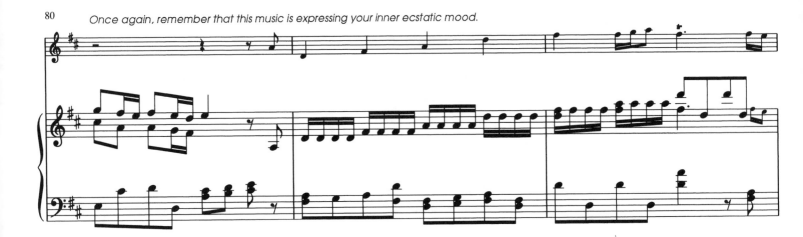

* *optional cadenza*

, rit. *brilliante* *a tempo*

harps _____ with gold - en wires.

rit. (col canto)

a tempo

Slightly accent the attack (from above) of the trill.

83

Let the bright Se - ra - phim in

Sing the appoggiatura on the beat, slightly accented.

86

burn - ing row,___ their

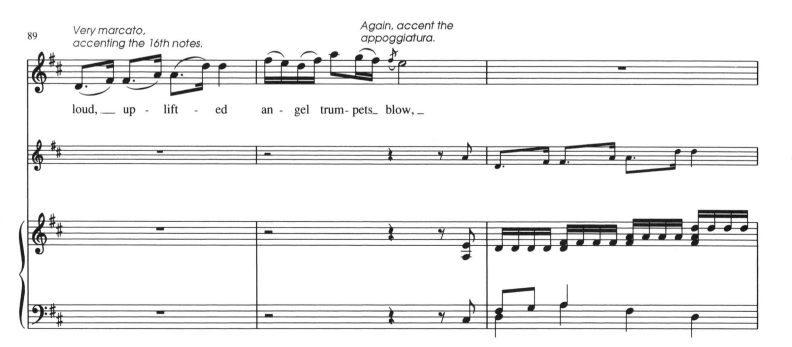

89

Very marcato, accenting the 16th notes.

Again, accent the appoggiatura.

loud,___ up - lift - ed an - gel trum - pets___ blow,___

92

*There should be a feeling of playful, heightened excitement
in all your da capo ornamentations.*

let the bright Se - ra - phim

in

95

burn - ing row, in burn - ing, burn - ing row, _ their

98

*Marcato. Try accenting
the 16th notes.*

*luftpause on
beat 4*

loud, up - lift - ed an - gel trum - pets blow, _____

p

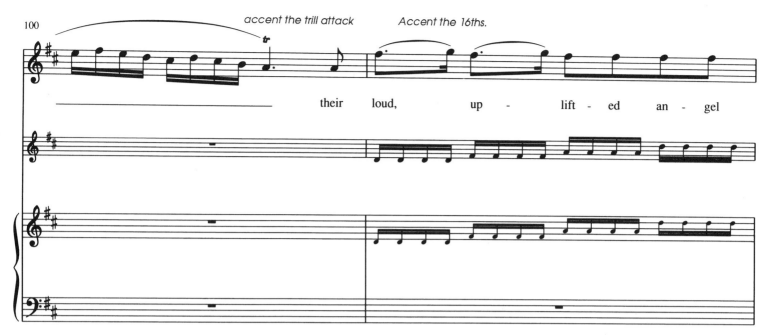

accent the trill attack   Accent the 16ths.

their loud,   up - lift - ed an - gel

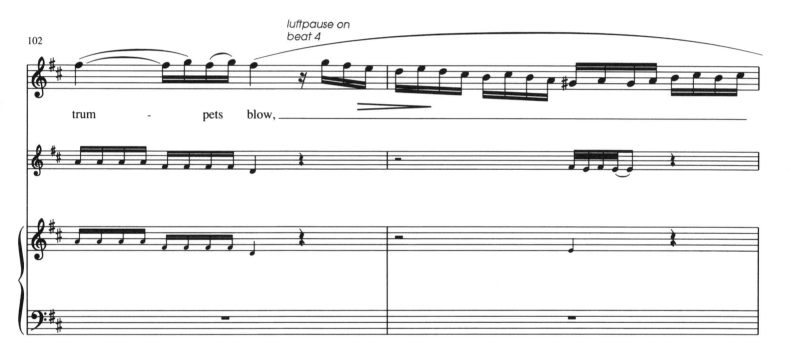

luftpause on
beat 4

trum - pets blow, _____

Keep the melisma energized, but the
beat steady.

cresc.

mf

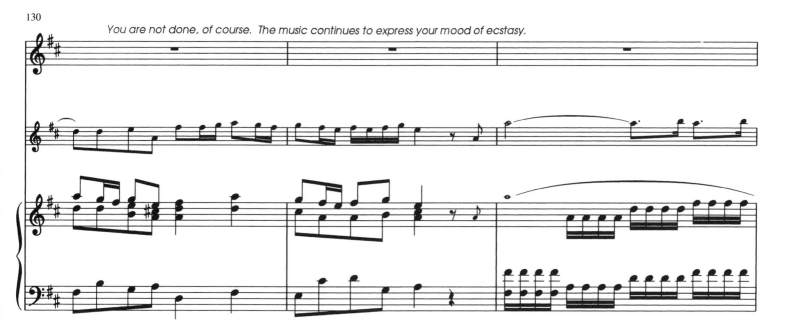

(This page left intentionally blank)

Let the bright Seraphim

from Samson

Trumpet in D

George Frideric Handel
Trumpet part edited
by Derek Stratton

The part may be carefully cut from the book

43

47

51

55

59

(tacet throughout B section)   *da capo*

17   3
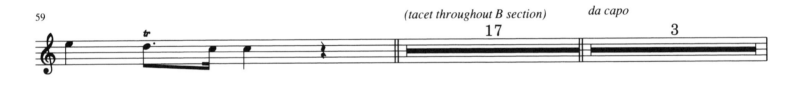

80

84

(voice re-enters)

2

89

93

3

98

101

104

107

111

115

120 **Slowly** *brilliante* **Tempo I**

124

127 *freely* *a tempo*

130

133

(This page left intentionally blank so that the part may be cut from the book.)

Ach, ich fühl's

from *Die Zauberflöte*
music by Wolfgang Amadeus Mozart

Setting: Legendary. At the temple of the sacred brotherhood.

In this fairytale *singspiel*, Pamina is crushed when her perfect lover, Tamino, will not speak to her, and avoids her completely. She does not realize that he is undergoing a series of trials as initiation into the brotherhood, and is currently under a vow of silence. Her fervent pleas test his loyalty to the oath.

This is an earnestly tragic aria, although there is little preparation for it in the story. Perhaps it will help you to remember that in this allegory, Pamina and Tamino are idealized, pure heroes. Their emotions are always clear and true. Look at how rapturously in love they were before they ever met! When Pamina feels that Tamino has rejected her, her love is so pure and her character so noble, that she has the full response of a classical tragic figure, like a dejected lover from a Greek tragedy. Listen to the dirge-like resignation in the orchestra part.

This noble, spun aria of Pamina's is pure Mozartean *bel canto*. To create its full musical effect, the voice should be pure, of an easy, caressing tone, without affectation, and intonation must be very accurate. There are some vocally difficult spots that will need careful attention by any soprano. The most difficult phrase is the long melisma on "Herzen" that begins in measure 14. Vocalism at this point must be the stylized expression of Pamina's longing. In performance this melisma cannot be merely a technical exercise. Take a breath before the first note of measure 14, and then keep the tempo steady throughout the melisma. Do not rush. If the tempo is rushed here, which singers are tempted to do, the nobility and restraint of Pamina's character suffers as a result. The scales must be even and beautiful. In measure 15, the notes marked staccato must not be too short. Just sing each of these four notes with the slightest hint of separation between them. They are the musical culmination of the melisma, Mozart's way of heightening the longing. Sing each of these four notes as if you want to hold onto something that is irrevocably slipping away. If the notes are too short they become meaningless.

Communicating Pamina's tragic rejection in a convincing way over the course of the aria is what is demanded of the singer. The character really feels as if all hope is lost and that life is over. You can only effectively sustain an emotion like this on stage if it is rooted in some sincere inner reality. Have you ever felt hopelessly sad at some point in your life? Remember all you can about that feeling, recalling the specifics and depth of how you felt. Conjure up all the details that you can remember to help you to recreate the emotion. Painful as it might be, this is what our art requires of us: honestly sharing our deepest selves through our performances. With some practice you can learn to apply real personal experience to your portrayals.

Ach, ich fühl's, es ist verschwunden,
ewig hin mein ganzes Glück,
ewig hin der Liebe Glück!
Nimmer kommt ihr, Wonnestunden,
    meinem Herzen mehr zurück.
Sieh, Tamino, diese Tränen fließen,
Trauter, dir allein.
Fühlst du nicht der Liebe Sehnen,
so wird Ruh im Tode sein.

Ah, I feel it; it has vanished—
forever gone, all my happiness,
forever gone, the happiness of love!
Never will you, blissful hours,
    come back again to my heart.
See, Tamino, these tears flow,
beloved one, for you alone.
If you do not feel the longing of love,
then peace will come to be in death.

Ach, ich fühl's

from *Die Zauberflöte*

Wolfgang Amadeus Mozart

*A deceptive cadence, followed by
renewed passion. Do not go too far out
of the vocal context by belting "fühlst du nicht."*

*The singer normally responds to the
dynamic of piano in the orchestra here.*

*Again, sing these arpeggiated melismas
very legato, emphasizing phrase, not notes.*

*Try a slight cresc.
on "so wird" before
the sub. pp on "Ruh."*

*Not too slowly on
the descent off the
fermata.*

No obvious chest voice.

*The violins in the orchestra seem to be saying
over and over, 'Tamino, Tamino."*

Deh vieni, non tardar

from *Le nozze di Figaro*
music by Wolfgang Amadeus Mozart

Setting: Near Seville, the 17th century. Count Almaviva's palace garden; night.

In Act IV of this complicated opera buffa, Susanna is in the garden disguised as her mistress, the Countess, in order to fool the Count into jealously thinking that the Countess has a planned rendezvous with Figaro. Of course, all the while the Countess is disguised as Susanna to expose the philandering of her husband, the Count, when he keeps his illicit date in the garden with someone whom he thinks is Susanna! Confused? As you can see, there's a wonderfully complex tangle at the climax of the Beaumarchais/Da Ponte story. And in the midst of this flurry comes this charming, quiet aria of Susanna's. I really recommend that anyone working on anything from "Figaro" should do some careful plot study to get a clear understanding of how all the details fit together. It is the only way to begin to build a character in this opera, which has some of the most vivid characters ever to grace the stage.

The aria is an amazing, sophisticated, subtle theatrical moment. It is unlike all the rest of Susanna's music in the opera, which tends to be action-oriented and generally bright. At this spot, Susanna (through Mozart's brilliant musical characterization) seems to try to imitate the Countess' restrained, cultivated style as part of the impersonation of her mistress. Notice how Mozart's genius keeps Susanna's ersatz nobility different (simpler, with less depth, and more self-conscious) from the Countess' true musical character. Compare this aria of Susanna's with the Countess' "Dove sono" and you can easily see the difference between this "pretend" nobility and the real thing. There is a touch of wit in the aria as well, since the whole scene is a charade, after all. We discover that the design of the scene is even richer when we realize that Susanna is actually singing "come, my love" to her eaves-dropping husband, Figaro, on their wedding night. Sincerely tender, sensuous longing is part of the rich texture of the scene.

How does one balance all of that in what appears to be a deceptively simple aria? There is only one way to try: you must know the whole opera, and you must understand who Susanna is.

This is often one of the first arias that a young soprano will sing, and it is a perfect opportunity for you to learn how to do research in preparing an aria. The opera is based on a famous play, which is readily available in paperback editions, and you should read Beaumarchais to get a concept of the character that is independent of the opera. It will show you what Mozart and Da Ponte started with, and give you a sense of what they brought to the character and story. You'll also want to read through the entire libretto of the opera, looking for clues to Susanna's character. You may want to listen to a recording of the entire opera to get a sense of the sweep and momentum of the score. Only after you have done considerable preparation will you be able to create the magical moment that this aria can be; otherwise it will never be anything more than a pleasant song. After your study, you won't be able to use everything you've learned about the character and the opera in this one brief aria, but it will give you a background on which to build the details of your performance. And don't be frustrated if it never feels as rich and full of meaning as when heard in the context of the opera. That's true of nearly every opera aria, but particularly one that relies on such a delicate interplay of plot and character. You can, however, do your best to summon up a 17th century Spanish night, to try and live and breathe as Susanna for a few minutes, and at least to convince the audience (and yourself) that you know what you're doing singing these sensuous phrases in Almaviva's garden.

Giunse alfin il momento,
    che godrò senza affanno
    in braccio all'idol mio.
Timide cure!
uscite dal mio petto;
a turbar non venite
il mio diletto!
Oh come par che
all'amoroso foco
l'amenità del loco,
la terra e il ciel
risponda,
come la notte
i furti miei seconda!

Deh vieni,
non tardar, o gioja bella.
Vieni ove amore
per goder t'appella
finchè non splende in ciel
    notturna face--
finchè l'aria è ancor bruna,
e il mondo tace.
Qui mormora il ruscel,
qui scherza l'aura,
    che col dolce susurro
    il cor ristaura,
qui ridono i fioretti
e l'erba è fresca.
Ai piaceri d'amor
tutto adesca.
Vieni, ben mio,
tra queste piante ascose!
Ti vo'la fronte incoronar
di rose.

The moment which I will enjoy
    without anxiety, in the arms of
    my idol, has finally arrived.
Timid feelings,
leave my breast;
don't come to disturb
my pleasure!
Oh, how it seems that
to amorous passion
the pleasantness of the place,
the earth, and the sky
respond,
as the darkness
favors my connivings!

Please come;
don't delay, oh beautiful joy.
Come to where love
calls you to enjoy yourself
until the nocturnal torch doesn't
    shine in the sky anymore—
until it's dark again,
and the world is still.
Here the stream murmurs;
here the breeze,
    which revives the heart with its
    gentle rustling, plays.
Here little flowers are laughing,
and the grass is fresh.
To the pleasures of love
everything is enticing.
Come, my dear,
among these sheltering trees!
I want to crown your head
with roses.

Deh vieni, non tardar

from *Le nozze di Figaro*

Wolfgang Amadeus Mozart

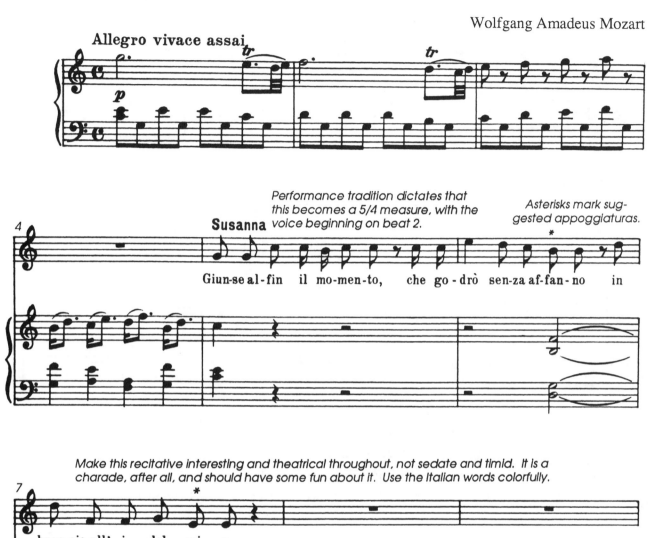

Performance tradition dictates that this becomes a 5/4 measure, with the voice beginning on beat 2.

Asterisks mark suggested appoggiaturas.

Susanna

Giun-se al-fin il mo-men-to, che go-drò sen-za af-fan-no in

Make this recitative interesting and theatrical throughout, not sedate and timid. It is a charade, after all, and should have some fun about it. Use the Italian words colorfully.

brac-cio all' i - dol mi - o.

The introduction and this interlude are good clues from Mozart of the delight of the situation.

Ti - mi-de cu - re! u -

40

Create a graceful arch to the phrase.

ta - ce.   Qui mor - mo - ra il ru -

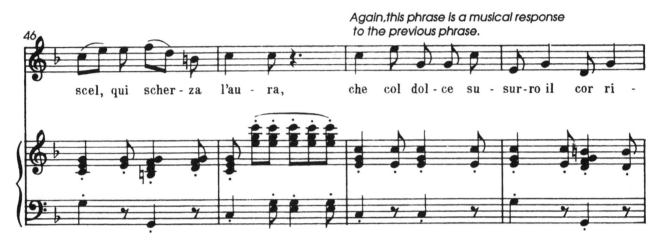

Again, this phrase is a musical response
to the previous phrase.

scel, qui scher - za l'au - ra,   che col dol - ce su - sur - ro il cor ri -

The introduction of dotted rhythms is a signal to sing with
added playfulness here. Begin the grace notes on the beat.

stau - ra,   qui ri - do - no i fio - ret - ti e l'er - ba è fre - sca,

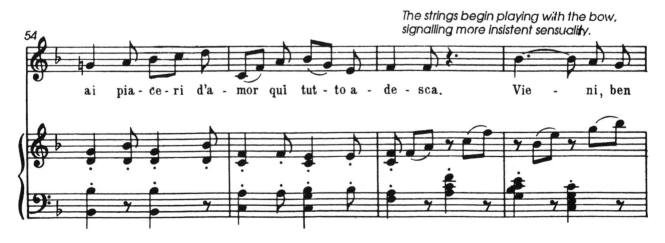

The strings begin playing with the bow,
signalling more insistent sensuality.

ai pia - ce - ri d'a - mor qui tut - to a - de - sca.   Vie - ni, ben

Vedrai, carino

from *Don Giovanni*
music by Wolfgang Amadeus Mozart

Setting: Seville, the 17th century. Night on a city street.

How interesting it is that both of Zerlina's arias have something to do with physical violence. In her first act aria, "Batti, batti," she seductively begs a suspicious and bewildered Masetto to beat her if he thinks she has been unfaithful to him. In a parallel duet scene later in Act II, Masetto actually has been beaten, whereupon Zerlina comforts and consoles her ailing beloved.

What a delight this simple aria is to sing! Vocally, it almost feels like one of the classic Italian arias of the 17th century that we all study. It invites the singer to work very consistently on sustaining an extremely legato line, with the melody constantly placed in a very resonant upper middle register of the voice. The music leaves the voice very exposed, requires careful intonation, and an evenness of tone. It's the kind of deceptively simple aria that looks as if there are no special challenges. However, once you get inside this piece, you will realize that it demands nothing less than perfection from you. Any flaws in your singing will be readily telegraphed to a listener.

The aria is marked *mezza voce,* and that presents some real challenges. I think that it will help to think of that marking as meaning not pianissimo, but simply a caressing, soothing tone that you would use to console someone. That will keep you from creating a tense or tentative sounding performance. An entire aria sung *mezza voce* can risk becoming very dull. One way to prevent that is to work very hard at the diction and meaning of the words to create new and exciting colors.

Another danger, especially when we are singing softly, is that the tempo may begin to drag. The remedy, I believe, is to feel the tempo in one, rather than in three. When we sing *mezza voce,* for some reason we sometimes tend to make late entrances. This drags the tempo down and takes the crispness away from a performance. (It will also drive a conductor crazy!) In nearly everything we sing, but this aria in particular, start each phrase in anticipation of the entrance. In the first entrance, for example, think of landing the first vowel sound of "e" on beat one, rather than placing the consonant sound of "v" right on beat one. If you start the "v" slightly before the beat it will insure that the vowel happens when it needs to. It will also create a necessary sense of urgency that any theatre music needs to be most effective. This slight anticipation will require a good deal of practice in order for you to feel comfortable with it. You will also probably notice that a by-product of this is that you will become much more aware of taking a good preparatory breath in launching a phrase.

Work diligently on the double consonants in spots like "sentilo battere" and "toccami qua" You should feel as if the double consonant actually stops the vowel sound in the voice for an instant. A well executed double consonant in Italian is the kind of detail that separates amateur singers from more seasoned professionals. In this aria, Mozart uses them very expressively, and you should sing them that way.

This is an aria of great tenderness and love, really almost a maternal kind of consoling. There is also a charming caressing quality as Zerlina sings to Masetto "toccami qua" Her strategy for healing this poor boy is not simply to stroke and console him, but also to say how much she loves him, and to offer herself to him in a loving, sensual way. She knows that will heal him faster than anything else!

We see here a quiet and very touching side to Zerlina's soubrette character. Even in a *mezza voce* aria, singing these quiet phrases of consolation, you should never forget the bright, energetic qualities of her character. In fact, it may help you to remember first and foremost her sparkling, vivacious charm. She doesn't lose that core to her character in this quiet scene. She simply shows a sweet and tender side of herself. Don't forget that she is very young, perhaps no more than 17 years old.

Vedrai, carino,	*You will see, dearest,*
se sei buonino,	*if you are good,*
che bel rimedio	*what fine medicine*
ti voglio dar.	*I want to give you.*
È naturale,	*It's natural.*
non da disgusto,	*It's not unpleasant;*
e lo speziale	*and the pharmacist*
non lo sa far,	*doesn't know how to make it—*
no, non lo sa far.	*no, he doesn't know how to make it.*
È un certo balsamo	*It's a certain balm*
che porto addosso.	*that I carry with me.*
Dare te'l posso,	*I can give it to you,*
se'l vuoi provar.	*if you want to try it.*
Saper vorresti	*Would you like to know*
dove mi sta?	*where I have it?*
Sentilo battere;	*Feel it beat;*
toccami quà.	*touch me here.*

Vedrai, carino

from *Don Giovanni*

Wolfgang Amadeus Mozart

Grazioso

The tempo should be in "one" rather than "three."

Mezza voce.

Anticipate the entrance; don't be late.

Grace notes start on the beat.

Sing very legato, mezza voce.

Zerlina:

Ve - drai, ca - ri - no, se sei buo - ni - no, che bel ri - me - di - o

Emphasize the downbeat on "dar," followed by a slight diminuendo.

The phrase builds to the third syllable of "naturale."

ti vo - glio dar! E na - tu - ra - le,

Phrase as before.

Resist the temptation to accent the "no's"

non dà di - sgu - sto, e lo spe - zia - le non lo sa far, no,

A slight cresc. or
decresc. will work on "far."
Experiment.

non lo sa far, no, non lo sa far.＿ E un cer - to bal-sa-mo

che por-to ad dos - so, da - re t'el pos - so, se il vuoi pro - var.＿

Use the double R to emphasize
the second syllable of "vorresti."

Sa - per vor - re - sti

slight crescendo   diminuendo

do - ve mi sta, do - ve, do - ve, do-ve mi sta?＿

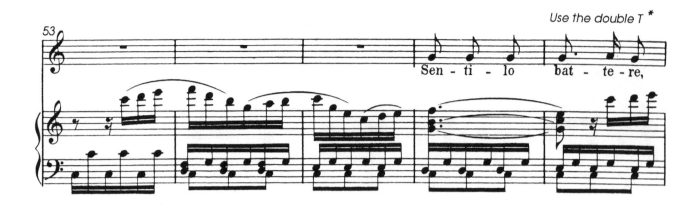

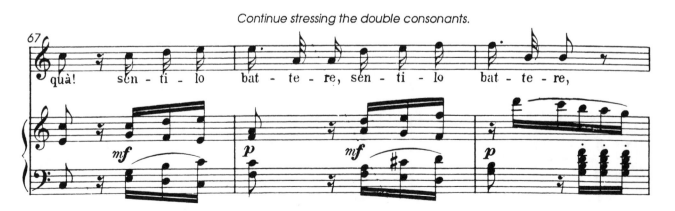

*Try this experiment: close the T sound on beat 2, holding the T for half a beat. The reason for this is to completely interrupt the vowel sound with an elongated consonant, which is foreign to us in English; we don't elongate consonants like this.

Don't sing an exaggerated portamento here.

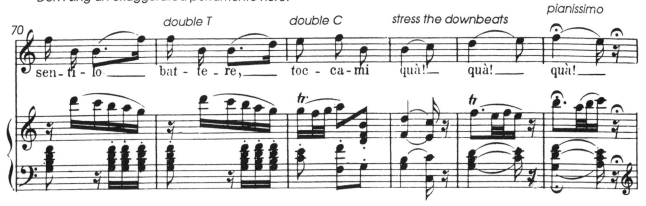

Batti, batti, o bel Masetto

from *Don Giovanni*
music by Wolfgang Amadeus Mozart

Setting: Seville, the 17th century. Late afternoon in Don Giovanni's palace garden.

Zerlina is a simple, lovely peasant girl, in love with her Masetto, and truly intending to marry him. However, she's impressionable, and in her own way, very sensual. The charms of the charismatic nobleman Don Giovanni nearly sway her to forget everything else and make love with him on her wedding day! This may seem outrageous (it's *meant* to be outrageous in the dramatic design of the opera), but just think of the Don as a glamourous celebrity, and remember that Zerlina is just an everyday peasant girl. If you were an impressionable, small town girl like Zerlina, and a handsome, alluring movie star suddenly walked into your life and swept you off your feet, even on your wedding day, wouldn't you be thrown off balance a little? Zerlina has a terrible time convincing Masetto that nothing actually happened with the Don, which is true enough. Her charm, intelligence, wit, and feminine strategies are shown very well in "Batti, batti" as she wins back Masetto's affection and trust.

Although we're starting right on the aria in this collection, which is the traditional way to perform the piece in concert, you might consider consulting the vocal score and adding a bit of the secco recitative before the aria. If you're having a difficult time feeling comfortable beginning the aria out of the blue, the recitative may help to put you at ease, and may help to motivate the opening of the aria.

Zerlina charms Masetto out of his jealousy. And how does she do that? By diffusing his anger with the ridiculous suggestion that he should go ahead and beat her. Ridiculous, because she knows him well, and knows that he's too gentle and loving to ever do such a thing to her. With her theatrical exaggeration and her wit, she disarms him of his jealousy. You should try this little scene in different attitudes: sarcastic and attacking, submissive, maternal, self-pitying, or sexually aggressive. As you ponder this, consider that underlying Zerlina's theatrical persuasion is the fact that she does feel just a little guilty and embarrassed about neglecting Masetto for Giovanni on their wedding day. So how does she deal with that guilt? By humorously saying, "O.K., go ahead and beat me!" Experiment with the character and scene as far as your imagination will take you as you step into Zerlina's shoes and respond to Mozart's music.

Many times in opera, musical details are the most important clues to the character and situation. Look at the point where the first section of the aria ends and the second section begins. Why did Mozart write it this way? Here's one way of looking at it. At the end of the first section, on the lines "Ah, lo vedo, non hai core," imagine that Zerlina knows that she's won, and just wants a smile out of Masetto as a concession. She's pressing her hand here, and is at her most coaxing and teasing. You could motivate that fermata on the last "core" with the thought that Zerlina is relishing the anticipation of Masetto's smile of concession. He can resist no longer, and at last cracks a smile, which is what happens in that brief little rest between sections. In fact, as an actress, it will help you if you think of that smile as the event that actually stops the music and launches the next section. Then, because Zerlina loves Masetto and really doesn't want to flaunt or analyze her victory, she goes right ahead into the cheerful reconciliation of the 6/8, singing with playful abandon and relief.

Do you see how carefully we can dig into operatic literature for performance details, and how exciting and interesting the aria becomes when we think through it like this? Of course, this is only my interpretation, but at least it shows the kind of investigation that is possible. You can add more depth to "Batti, batti" by studying Zerlina's other aria, "Vedrai, carino."

Zerlina is a theatrical cousin to Susanna in *Figaro*. Her role isn't as prominent nor as developed in *Don Giovanni*, nor is Zerlina as resourceful as Susanna, but both roles are for exactly the same type of voice and character in a soprano (as is their other Mozart cousin, Despina of *Così fan tutte*). This type of role is rooted in the *commedia dell'arte* tradition. One need only look at Pergolesi's *La Serva Padrona* for a more traditional, purer stereotype of this same "soubrette" character. Mozart transcended that stock buffa type, breathing rich new life into into Zerlina, Despina and Susanna. They are the most attractive and fun-loving women in his operas. Even if you don't feel that you are a quintessential soubrette type, every young soprano can benefit by working on these arias.

Batti, o bel Masetto,
la tua povera Zerlina.
Starò qui come agnellina
   le tue botte ad aspettar.
L'ascerò straziarmi il crine,
l'ascerò cavarmi gli occhi,
e le care tue manine lieta poi
   saprò baciar.
Ah, lo vedo, non hai core:

Pace, o vita mia;
in contenti ed allegria
notte e dì vogliam passar,
sì, sì...

Hit, oh handsome Masetto,
your poor Zerlina.
Like a little lamb
   I'll await your blows.
I'll let my hair be pulled out.
I'll let my eyes be scratched out.
And then, happy, I will be able to kiss
   your dear beloved hands.
Ah, I see it: you don't have courage!

Peace, oh love of my life!
In contentment and good cheer
 let's enjoy passing the nights and days.
Yes, yes...

Batti, batti, o bel Masetto
from *Don Giovanni*

Wolfgang Amadeus Mozart

*Be certain that you are vocally and mentally prepared for the first note before
you even begin the aria.*

Use no portamento; make clean attacks.

The phrase moves forward to the downbeat of the next measure.

Inner thoughts continue flowing between the rests.

Lascie-rò straziar mi il cri-ne,

Delicately shape these two-note slurs,

Lascie-rò cavar-mi gli occhi, e le ca - re tue ma -

but also make them part of the longer phrase.

Slightly accent and separate the 32nd notes for clarity of articulation.

ni - ne lie - ta poi sa-prò ba - ciar, sa - prò ba -

Slightly stress appoggiaturas.

ciar, ba - ciar, sa - prò, sa - prò ba -

There should be some fun and heightened excitement in singing this melodically decorated recapitulation of the first section. Find a subtext and a way of motivating the "frills."

ciar.   Bat - ti, __ batti, o __ bel Ma -

set - to, la __ tua po - ve - ra Zer - li - na! sta - rò qui come a - gnel -

yearning

li - na le tue botte ad a - spet - tar.   O bel Ma - sèt - to!

Don't forget the double T's.

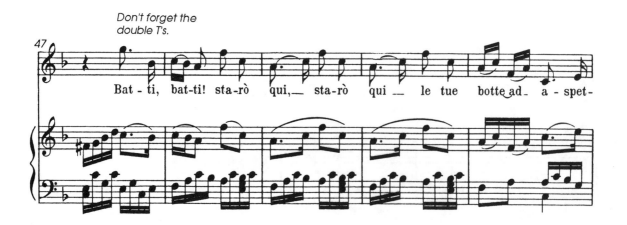

Bat - ti, bat - ti! sta - rò qui, __ sta - rò qui __ le tue botte ad __ a - spet -

slight cresc.; stress the downbeat

tar.   Ah,   lo ve - do,

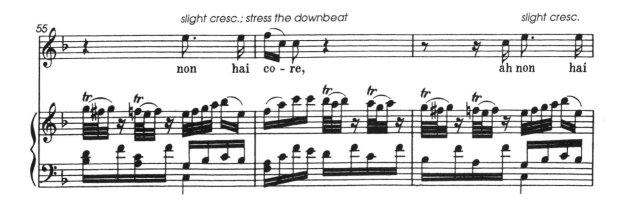

slight cresc.; stress the downbeat   *slight cresc.*

non   hai co - re,   ah non   hai

This whole line should be thought of as one phrase, building to a climax before the tempo change.   * *(see footnote)*   *Sing the built-in arch in each phrase.*

Allegro.

co - re, ah,   lo ve - do, non   hai co - re.   Pa - ce, pa - ce, o vi - ta

Try to create long legato lines, contrasting the fast moving notes in the accompaniment.

mi - a!   pa - ce, pa - ce, o vi - ta   mi - a! in__ con - ten - to, ed al - le -

See the companion essay about motivating the tempo change. A new vocal color (brighter and more joyful) should be heard in this section.

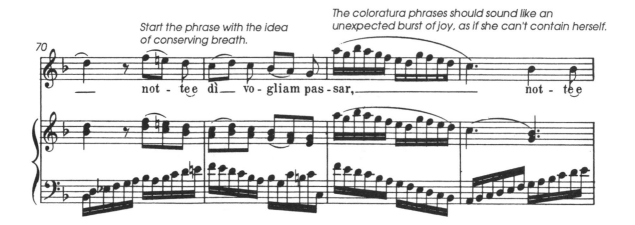

stress the downbeat

mi - - a! in con - ten - to ed al - le - - gri - a not - te e

Slightly separate the notes on "si."   *cresc. to the downbeat*

dì — vo - gliam pas - sar, sì, sì, sì, sì, sì, sì, not - te e

Breathe here to stress the "si."   *cresc. to the downbeat*

dì — vo - gliam pas - sar, sì, sì, sì, sì, sì, sì, not - te e dì — vo - gliam pas-

sar, _____ vo - gliam, vo - gliam pas - sar, _____ vo - gliam, vo - gliam pas-

The final cut-off should be a crisp flipped R.

sar.

pp

O wär' ich schon mit dir vereint

from *Fidelio*
music by Ludwig van Beethoven

Setting: Seville, the 18th century. The courtyard of the prison fortress.

Marzelline's father, Rocco, is the jailer of the state prison. For some time she has been courted by Jacquino, the porter at the prison, and at one time she was fond of him. But her feelings for Jacquino have cooled. She has fallen head over heels in love with Fidelio, Rocco's new assistant. (Fidelio is actually Leonora, in disguise as a young man, who has taken the job at the prison to work for the escape of her captive husband, Florestan.) In the duet that opens the opera, and directly precedes the aria, we see Jacquino nervously proposing, and Marzelline firmly refusing his amorous offers. She's not a hard-hearted flirt, though. In asides to the audience, she says that she must be firm, and that it's the kindest thing to do under the circumstances. She knows how Jacquino suffers, since she herself loves one who has not returned her affection. The aria begins after Jacquino's exit, and we hear Marzelline swoon with love for Fidelio.

Marzelline is a variation of the familiar soubrette character from the 18th century, although she is more prosaic and earthbound than some of her stage predecessors. In thinking about her character, imagine that she lives in a rather rough, unpleasant world that revolves around prison life. She is the only woman on the premises. It's not hard to imagine why she falls so hard for Fidelio. She lives among coarse men, and is drawn to him because of his grace and natural tenderness. Of course, she doesn't know that those soft qualities are because "he" is actually a "she!" In her aria she doesn't seem to be a Spanish girl at all, but very much a German one, dreaming of peaceful domesticity and the happiness that diligent work brings.

This aria should be no mystery to most young women. Many of us dream, fall in love, and hope to marry the man of our dreams. We may daydream about life with him, living together in a home of our own, just as Marzelline dreams of her life with Fidelio. She's a very discreet girl of 1805, but there are hints of her sensuous desire when she says, "a young girl must admit to only half of what she is thinking." That restrained sensual longing is part of her daydream.

The emotional challenge of the aria is to find those sincere, real feelings in yourself that correspond to Marzelline, and make them your own. Though the character communicates her feelings in a stylized way, her longings are deep and heartfelt. Even though you're singing a German text to Beethoven's music of nearly 200 years ago, the aria should have the same genuineness as if you were confiding these feelings to a trusted friend in present day American vernacular.

O wär' ich schon mit dir vereint,
und dürfte Mann dich nennen!
Ein Mädchen darf ja, was es meint,
    zur Hälfte nur bekennen!
Doch wenn ich nicht erröthen muß
ob einem warmen Herzenskuß,
wenn nichts uns stört auf Erden...
Die Hoffnung schon erfüllt die Brust
Mit unaussprechlich süßer Lust;
wie glücklich will ich werden!

In Ruhe stiller Häuslichkeit
erwach' ich jeden Morgen.
Wir grüssen uns mit Zärtlichkeit;
der Fleiss verscheucht die Sorgen.
Und ist die Arbeit abgethan,
dann schleicht die holde Nacht heran;
dann ruh'n wir von Beschwerden.

Wie will ich glücklich werden!

Oh, were I already united with you,
and could call you husband!
A young girl must, of course, admit to
    only half of what she is thinking!
But, when I won't have to blush
because of a warm, caressing kiss,
when nothing on earth will disturb us...
Hope already fills my breast
with unspeakably sweet pleasure.
How happy I will be!

In the quiet of peaceful domesticity
I will wake up each morning.
We will greet each other with tenderness;
diligent work will drive away anxieties.
And when the work is put aside,
then lovely night will descend;
then we will rest from cares.

How happy I will be!

O wär' ich schon mit dir vereint

from *Fidelio*

Ludwig van Beethoven

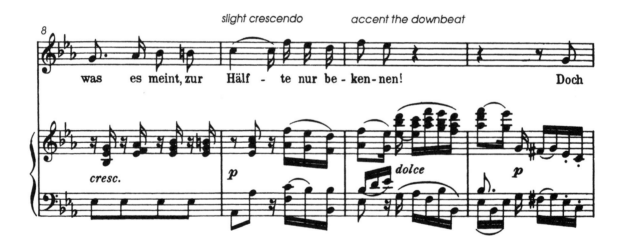

*she blushes, and can't
even finish her sentence*

*Pay attention to pick up notes.
Really sing them, and in tune.*

uns stört auf Er - den _____   Die

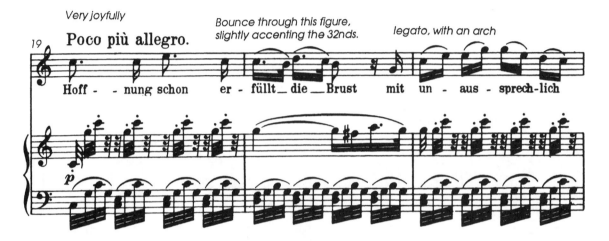

Very joyfully

Poco più allegro.

*Bounce through this figure,
slightly accenting the 32nds.*

legato, with an arch

Hoff - - nung schon er - füllt _ die _ Brust mit un - aus - sprech - lich

*The phrase builds to the
high G, then relaxes.*

sü - - sser _ Lust;   wie glück - lich will ich wer - den, wie glück - lich will ich

Don't drop the phrase here.

wer - den!   Die Hoff - nung schon er - füllt die

Give a very pronounced final "t" *as before*

Brust mit un-aus-sprech - lich sü-sser Lust; wie glücklich, glücklich, ja wie

cresc.

accent the downbeat

glück - lich will ich wer - den!

sfp *cresc.* *f* *sf* *p*

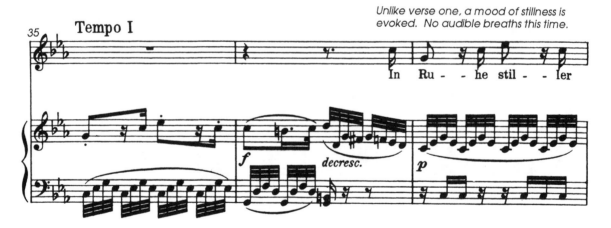

Tempo I

Unlike verse one, a mood of stillness is evoked. No audible breaths this time.

In Ru - - he stil - - ler

f *decresc.* *p*

As if in a daydream

Häus - - lich-keit er - wach' ich je - - den Mor - - - gen, wir

cresc. *sf* *p*

grü - ssen uns mit Zärt - lich-keit, der Fleiss_____ verscheucht die

Sor - gen. Und ist die Ar - beit

ab - ge-than, dann schleicht die hol - de____ Nacht her-an, dann ruh'n

wir von Be-schwer-den. Die

The joy of the second refrain is more exuberant than the first.

53 Poco più allegro.

Hoff - nung schon er - füllt__ die__ Brust mit un - aus - sprech-lich__

Enjoy the dotted rhythms.   *The phrase builds to the G, then relaxes.*

56

sü - sser Lust; wie glück-lich will ich wer - den, wie glück - lich will ich

cresc.   *sfp*

These phrases are energetic outbursts.

59

wer - den! Die Hoff - nung schon er-füllt die

dolce

Brust _ _ _ _ mit un-aus-sprech - lich sü-sser Lust; wie glücklich, glücklich, ja wie

cresc.

*This time, rather than relaxing the phrase
after the G, keep the momentum
going into the tempo change.*

The "coda" should have a heightened excitement.

Più mosso.

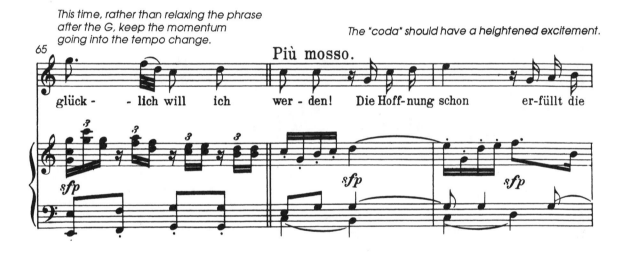

glück - - lich will ich wer - den! Die Hoff-nung schon er-füllt die

sfp   _sfp_   _sfp_

subito piano, then cresc.

Brust _ _ mit un - aus-sprech - lich sü - sser Lust; _____

cresc. poco a poco

wie will ich

glück - lich, wie will ich glück - lich__ wer - - den,

*In the little free cadenza she is
suddenly quiet and reflective. . .then bright and
exuberant again.*

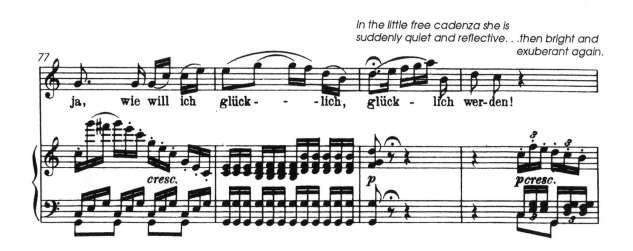

ja, wie will ich glück - - lich, glück - lich wer-den!

Ah! Je veux vivre

from *Roméo et Juliette*
music by Charles Gounod

Setting: Verona, the 16th century. A ball at the Capulet palace; evening.

The aria really has no counterpart scene in Shakespeare's famous play. In the play, Juliet is talked about a great deal before the ball scene. Her mother and nurse discuss marriage with the girl, to which Juliet briefly replies that she's not given it much thought: "It is an honour that I dream not of." In both these scenes, much is made of her young age of thirteen, and also that in Verona this is the age that girls can respectably marry. (Thank goodness times have changed!) At the ball, Shakespeare's Juliet meets Romeo in a brief, enchanted conversation, but nowhere does she extol the joy of being young and free, as she does in the opera. Gounod and his librettists have invented this moment for Juliet probably to establish her bright, vivacious character (and also maybe to give the leading soprano a good entrance aria). Whatever the origins, it's one of the best French arias that a young soprano can have in her repertory.

This is a bright, youthful, ebullient burst of song. Think of her as a dreamy, energetic adolescent who's at an age when she's just getting a sense of who she is. In the opera (though not in the play), the ball is being held in celebration of Juliet's birthday, which adds to her joyful reflection that "this rapture of youth only lasts a day." She's aware that her family expects her to marry soon, but in the aria she feels too giddy to want to think of settling down as someone's wife. (Of course, she doesn't know that she will meet Romeo in a few minutes and long to be his wife immediately.)

The aria is full of difficulties. The opening line is a mine field of potential intonation problems. The descending, a capella, chromatic scale must be sung exactly on pitch, and this is very difficult. You must hear an exact half-step interval between each note in the scale. It's easy to sing half-steps that are far too wide or too small. One result might be, of course, that you wind up on the wrong note at the end of the phrase. Beyond that, if you sing this opening "fanfare" phrase out of tune, you have negated the bright, crisp mood of the aria right off the bat. Even after you have built the aria into your voice, in performance you will always have to work hard to consciously tune this phrase. A spot like this can never run on "automatic pilot." The same kind of concentrated effort is needed in measures 101-104.

An appropriate musical exercise I can suggest is that in the practice room you might actually dance a carefee little waltz to the music. It's a good thing to do in working on any piece that is essentially dance music. If you can move lightly, easily, and gracefully to the music, it can help you to sing with those qualities, too. It might also help you to achieve the lighthearted feeling of abandon that the aria needs.

Because of performance expectations, you really must take the optional high run in measure 75. To do this phrase as originally written would probably be unacceptable in today's auditions and performances. And even though Gounod did not write a high C at the end of the aria, this has become expected as well. However, the optional ornaments and high notes in measures 117-120 do not necessarily need to be sung for a good performance of the aria. There are some sopranos for whom this aria is appropriate, but who cannot successfully "pop" these high notes in this style of coloratura. It's not only a matter of acquired vocal agility, it's also a matter of natural voice type. Some voices will probably never do this kind of frilly fun very easily. When it comes to this spot, my advice is: "If you've got it, flaunt it—if you don't, don't worry about it."

Ah! Je veux vivre dans le rêve
qui m'enivre ce jour encor!
Douce flamme, je te garde
dans mon âme comme un trésor!

Ah! Je veux vivre dan le rêve…

Cette ivresse de jeunesse
ne dure, hélas! qu'un jour.
Puis vient l'heure où l'on pleure;
le cœur cède à l'amour,
et le bonheur fuit sans retour!

Ah! Je veux vivre dans le rêve
qui m'enivre longtemps encor!
Loin de l'hiver morose
laisse-moi sommeiller
et respirer la rose
avant de l'effeuiller.

Ah! Douce flamme,
reste dans mon âme
comme un doux trésor
longtemps encor!

Ah! I want to live in the dream
which still intoxicates me on this day!
Gentle flame, I keep you
in my soul as a treasure!

Ah! I want to live in the dream…

This rapture of youth
only lasts, alas, a day.
After that comes the hour when one weeps;
the heart gives way to love,
and happiness flies away, never to return!

Ah! I want to live in the dream,
which intoxicates me, for a long time still!
Far from gloomy winter
let me slumber
and inhale the rose
before its petals fall.

Ah! Gentle flame,
stay in my soul
as a sweet treasure
for a long time still!

Ah! Je veux vivre

from *Roméo et Juliette*

Charles Gounod

Tempo di Valzer animato

This opening melisma represents a joyous burst of laughter.

Ah!

68

dans mon â - - me_____ Com - - me un tré -

sor!_____ Je veux vi - - vre_____

Dans ce rê - - ve_____ qui m'en - -

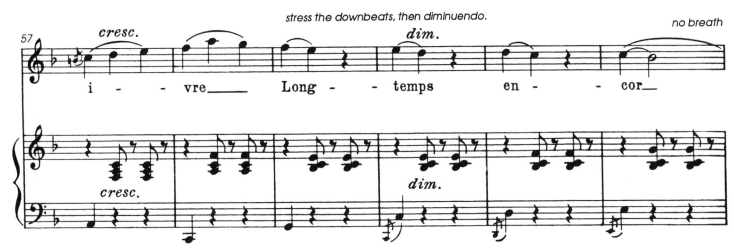

i - - vre_____ Long - - temps en - - cor_____

74

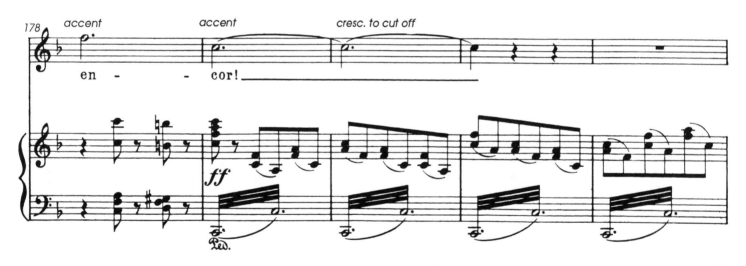

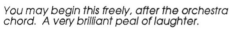

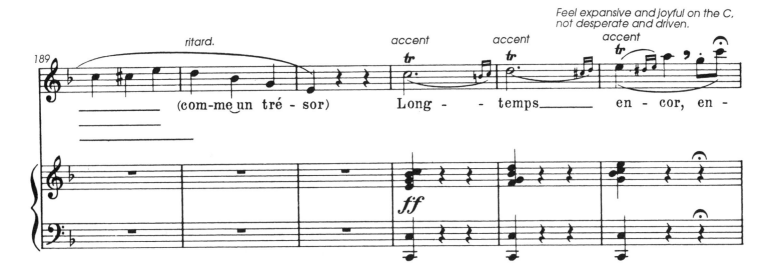

Mi chiamano Mimì

from *La bohème*
music by Giacomo Puccini

Setting: Paris, 1830. A garret apartment in the Latin quarter; Christmas Eve.

Here is a brief plot set-up for this aria from this most famous of operas:

Mimi's candle has gone out, and she has no way to light it. She knocks on the first available door in the hallway in her apartment building. Rodolfo as he answers the door. Just inside his apartment, she faints and is revived by Rodolfo with a sprinkle of water and a sip of wine. Rodolfo lights her candle, and she leaves. But in the hallway she realizes that she has somehow lost her apartment key while in Rodolfo's garret. The draft from the open door blows out her candle again, and his candle also goes out (Was this a purposeful accident?) In the dark of the garret they search for the key. Rodolfo finds it, but because he finds Mimi charming and doesn't want her to leave, he hides the key and pretends to continue looking. He strategically comes near to her, and as they touch he takes her hand and says that there is no use in looking any further. It's just too dark. He tells her all about himself, and then asks Mimi to tell him who she is and what she does.

In Rodolfo's aria ("Che gelida manina") that precedes Mimi's, he paints an affecting picture of himself as a poet living in happy poverty, rich with hopes, dreams and castles in the air. And then, just when he knows he's charmed her, he poetically tells Mimi that all his dreams were stolen away by two thieves, her eyes. At that point he implores her to speak to him.

Well, with the expansive rhetorical mood set by Rodolfo, Mimi isn't likely to toss off a quick recital of vital statistics about herself. She follows his lead and indulges in a rather long discourse about what she does and how she feels about things. She is clearly attracted to Rodolfo, flirts with him a little, and enjoys his attention. Beyond that, there seems to be an instant connection of intimacy between them that emboldens her to reveal so much to him in their first minutes together.

There is a great deal that can be read between the lines in this first meeting of Mimi and Rodolfo, all of which will vary with each person's interpretation. But just to get you started on your own course, ask yourself these questions: Could it be that there is a reason for Mimi choosing this particular apartment to go to for help? Is it so unlikely that she has seen the fellows that live there coming and going, or perhaps heard them in their sometimes wild antics? Is it possible that it wasn't accidental that Mimi left the key in Rodolfo's apartment? By thinking about the character and her situation in this way, and imagining what has led to the moment of this aria, you will come up with your own perfectly valid interpretation. Remember, write your own subtext always.

Mimi is one of the richest characters in opera, and certainly one of the best known, but there is much that is a mystery about her. She doesn't tell us much about her past, so we must draw our own conclusions by pondering what she tells us. She seems to be all alone in Paris, without evidence of or reference to family or close friends. Perhaps she has recently moved to the city, or is an orphan, or has recently broken with a lover, or is estranged from her family for some reason—there are lots of possible reasons for her apparent aloneness. She is intelligent, with an artistic nature, but is probably uneducated, and makes a living as a seamstress, as well as embroidering special lilies and roses as a hobby. The character shows an interesting mixture of self-reliance and fragility, combining a practical common sense with a wistful daydreaminess.

Puccini is a very exacting composer for the voice. He gives us many indications and clues in the score for our performances, and in preparing any Puccini aria we need to pay careful attention to all his markings.

Too often singers disregard too many of these specifics. The aria is so famous that it seems it has been performed and recorded by virtually every soprano who ever set foot on a stage. We must be careful to work out our own ideas about a piece, and not simply parrot performances by others, even the most revered and famous. The important thing is that you don't simply borrow someone else's way of doing things; it will never feel nor sound like your own.

The key to successfully performing this aria, after fully researching the character and situation in great detail, and after fully preparing the piece vocally and musically, is to present it in an unaffected, sincere and honest way. This is a character and situation that all young women should be able to relate to in a very personal way. Keep it on that level. Don't struggle to make affected, grand opera out of it. Keep it simple.

Sì. Mi chiamano Mimì,	*Yes… They call me Mimi,*
ma il mio nome è Lucia.	*but my name is Lucia.*
La storia mia è breve:	*My story is brief:*
A tela o a seta	*On linen or on silk*
ricamo in casa e fuori.	*I do embroidery at home and outside.*
Son tranquilla e lieta,	*I am quiet and cheerful,*
ed è mio svago far gigli e rose.	*and my hobby is making lilies and roses.*
Mi piaccion quelle cose	*Those things give me pleasure*
che han sì dolce malìa,	*which have so much sweet charm,*
che parlano d'amor, di primavere,	*which speak of love, of springtimes,*
che parlano di sogni e di chimere--	*which speak of dreams and of fantasies—*
quelle cose che han nome poesia.	*those things which are called poetry.*
Lei m'intende?	*Do you understand me?*
Mi chiamano Mimì.	*They call me Mimi.*
Il perchè non so.	*Why, I don't know.*
Sola, mi fo il pranzo da me stessa.	*Alone, I make meals at home by myself.*
Non vado sempre a messa	*I do not always go to mass*
ma prego assai il Signor.	*but I pray a great deal to the Lord.*
Vivo sola, soletta,	*I live alone—all alone—*
là in una bianca cameretta;	*there, in a clean little room;*
guardo sui tetti e in cielo.	*I look out on the rooftops and the sky.*
Ma quando vien lo sgelo	*But when the spring thaw comes*
il primo sole è mio…	*the early sun is mine…*
il primo bacio dell'aprile è mio!	*the first kiss of April is mine!*
Germoglia in un vaso una rosa…	*A rose blooms in a vase…*
foglia a foglia la spio!	*petal by petal I watch over it!*
Così gentil il profumo d'un fior!	*How delicate, the scent of a flower!*
Ma i fior ch'io faccio, ahimè!	*But the flowers that I make, alas,*
non hanno odore!	*do not have fragrance!*
Altro di me non le saprei narrare.	*I would not know how to tell you anything else about me.*
Sono la sua vicina	*I am your neighbor*
che la vien fuori d'ora a importunare.	*who comes unexpectedly to interrupt you.*

Mi chiamano Mimì

from *La bohème*

Giacomo Puccini

In your dramatic inner life, motivate for yourself the change of mood and the launching into a new section in m. 15. The 16th rest before "mi placcion" is dramatically most significant.

Son tran-quil-la e lie - ta ed è mio sva-go far gi-gli e. ro - se.__ Mi

Mimi becomes comfortable enough to leave the bare facts and talk about her feelings. The singing style goes from recitative to arioso.

Andante calmo ♩ = 54

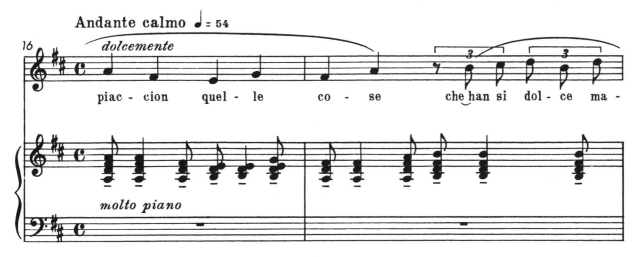

piac - cion quel - le co - se che han si dol - ce ma -

The rit. really translates into a fermata on the high A. Modify the i (ee) vowel to i as in "him."

lì - a, che par - la-no d'a-mor, di pri-ma-ve - re,_____

80

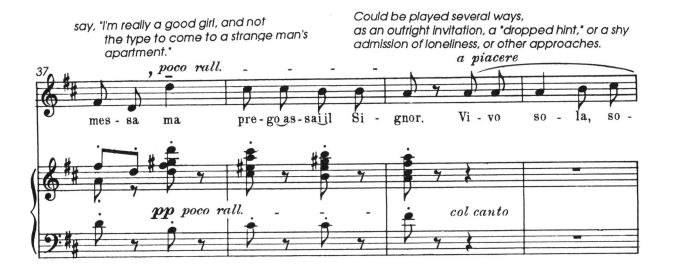

say, "I'm really a good girl, and not
the type to come to a strange man's
apartment."

Could be played several ways,
as an outright invitation, a "dropped hint," or a shy
admission of loneliness, or other approaches.

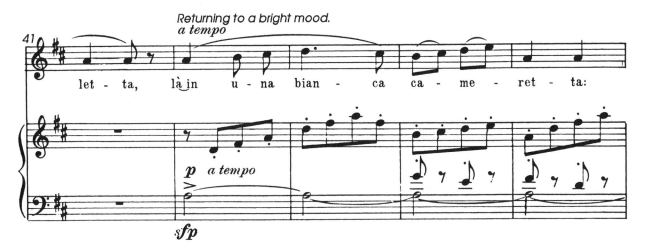

Returning to a bright mood.

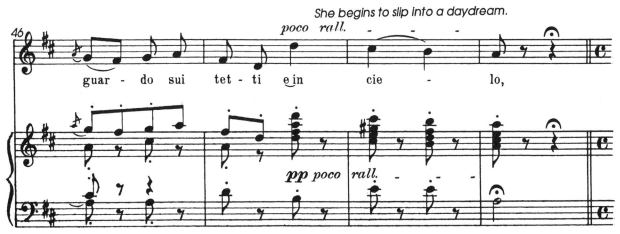

She begins to slip into a daydream.

Lost in her thoughts, as if in a daydream—less aware of Rodolfo, and feeling
free enough with him to rhapsodize like this.

Performance tradition puts a tenuto on the high A.

il primo bacio dell'aprile è

This repetion of the words is a more introverted reflection
than the first statement in the previous phrase.

il primo sole è mio! Ger-

Her poetic mood continues into this new section, returning to the subject of flowers and repeating the
flower music, but with more passion and confidence this time.

mogliain un va-souna ro-sa... Fogliaa foglia la spio! Così gen-

It's not necessary, but you might try a pianissimo on the high A.

This thought is the most profound poetical/philosophical statement of the whole aria.

Becoming self-conscious once again. Sing with conversational inflection.

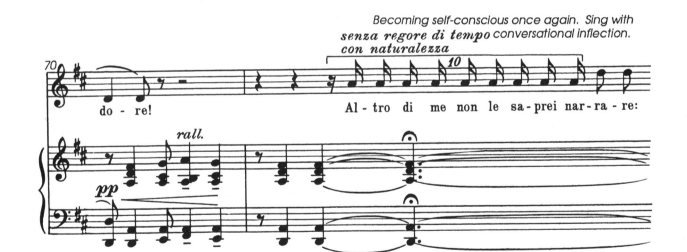

Don't come out of character too quickly at the end of the aria.

Quando men vo

from *La bohème*

music by Giacomo Puccini

Setting: Paris, 1830. Café Momus in the Latin Quarter; Christmas Eve.

Marcello, the painter, and Musetta, the cafe singer, have had a stormy, on-again-off-again romance. They always seem to be coming back together, only to break up again. They are both very emotional, impetuous individuals, and the sparks certainly fly between them (which is what makes their relationship both exciting and difficult). We hear about Musetta, though not by name, before she even sets foot on stage. Marcello barks some bitter remarks about love, and Rodolfo tells Mimì that his friend is nursing a broken heart. Musetta must be somewhat of a celebrity in the Latin Quarter, notorious for her beauty, her bold theatricality, her frivolity, her independence, her coquettish charm, and her irresistible power over men. She's at least enough of a local celebrity to elicit wide-eyed gossip from all those present as she very conspicuously enters the café, dressed to kill, and treating her escort, the old Alcindoro, like a pet poodle. After she plops Alcindoro and herself down at the table next to Marcello, Rodolfo, Mimi, Schaunard and Colline, she becomes annoyed when the party ignores her. More particularly, she craves Marcello's attention. Trying to force him to acknowledge her, she jumps up and shouts at the waiter that the plate in front of her smells dirty, and she crashes it to the floor amid rantings and ravings. She becomes bolder and bolder in focusing her attention on Marcello, who remains purposefully unresponsive. Being a café singer by profession, she suddenly bursts into this amusing, exaggerated, unashamedly narcissistic waltz song, directing the whole performance in Marcello's direction. As all the other characters later comment, Musetta is most definitely in love with Marcello.

The aria is full of subtleties that are key to its seductive tone. Musetta is a natural, extroverted performer, and she is at the peak of her form in this scene. There must be an exaggerated theatricality about it, motivated not only by her desire to be the center of attention, but also by her love for Marcello. All of Puccini's specific markings (*con molta grazia ed eleganza, quasi ritardando, appena allargando*, etc.) must be carefully observed. There are more musical indications of this nature in this four-page aria than in any other piece of comparable length that comes to mind. Puccini has given perfect directions that will motivate the entire aria if you seriously consider and employ all his indications. If you ignore them, the aria will never have the seductive, playful energy that it needs.

Nearly every soprano, regardless of voice type, winds up singing this piece. Perhaps it's because it's a perfect aria for auditions. It's short, it has lots of character, it has the kind of tessitura that flatters the voice, and has three good high notes. In closing, I think it will help you to remember that although Musetta is performing this song in a room full of strangers, it is really a private seduction of Marcello in a public arena.

Quando men vo soletta per la via	*When I go out alone in the street*
la gente sosta e mira…	*people stop and stare…*
e la bellezza mia tutta ricerca in me	*and they all study my beauty*
da capo a piè.	*from head to foot.*
Ed assaporo allor la bramosia sottil	*And then I savor the subtle longing*
che da gl'occhi traspira;	*that comes from their eyes;*
e dai palesi vezzi intender sa	*they know how to appreciate, beneath*
alle occulte beltà.	*obvious charms, all the hidden beauty.*
Così l'effluvio del desìo	*Thus the flow of desire*
tutta m'aggira;	*completely surrounds me;*
felice mi fa!	*it makes me happy!*
E tu che sai, che memori	*And you who know, who remember*
e ti struggi,	*and are melting with passion—*
da me tanto rifuggi?	*you avoid me so?*
So ben: le angoscie tue	*I know well: your sufferings—*
non le vuoi dir;	*you don't want to tell them;*
so ben,	*I know well,*
ma ti senti morir!	*but you feel like you're dying!*

Quando men vo

from *La bohème*

Giacomo Puccini

trip through the grace notes

pull it back, then
cresc. molto

expansively and exaggerated; theatrical

Turning her attention directly
to Marcello. More intimate.

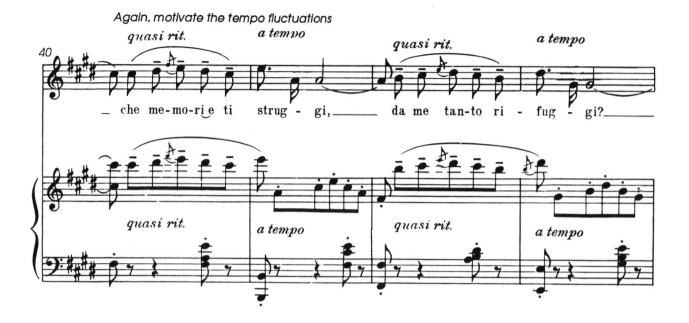

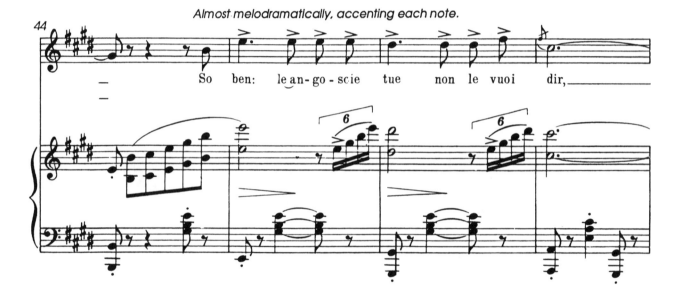